# THIS
# BOOK
## OF
# DREAMS
## AND
# SHADOWS

### IS THE SACRED TOOL OF:

_Elizabeth Violo_

# THE
# BOOK
## OF
# DREAMS
## AND
# SHADOWS

## A WITCH'S TOOL

### LADY RAYA

WEISER BOOKS
Boston, MA/York Beach, ME

First published in 2001 by
Red Wheel/Weiser, LLC
P. O. Box 612
York Beach, ME 03910-0612

Printed in the United States of America
ISBN 1-57863-250-1

MV

08 07 06 05 04 03 02 01
8 7 6 5 4 3 2 1

The paper used in this publication meets the minimum requirements of
the American National Standard for Information Sciences—Permanence
of Paper for Printed Library Materials Z39.48-1992 (R1997).

# The Book of Dreams and Shadows

A private journal for the keeping of secrets is a primary tool for the working witch. In this book, you will record your rhymes and rituals to use in your sacred circle. You will also keep this book, along with a special pen, by your bedside at night to record your dreams. The pen you use should be reserved for writing in your *Book of Dreams and Shadows* only. When you are not using your book, wrap it in a silk cloth and keep it private and secure in a secret location. Never show what you have written here to anyone. These dreams and rituals are your conversations with ~~God~~. the Great Spirit

## To Prepare Your Book for Use

To consecrate your book and make it holy for its sacred duty, first cleanse it of any aura but your own. To do this, place the book on a clean, soft cloth. If you can, it would be best to light a white candle and burn frankincense incense or essential oil. Sweep the air clear around your book with a sweet-smelling twig from a plant such as pine or mint. Say, as you are doing this:

> *Forces against me, unfriendly beings, be gone from this book, my tool.*
> *Clear and perfect, form around me, Teacher, Scribe, and Fool.*
> *May this book be granted the talent to guide me,*
> *in the Name and by the Hand of my Creator.*
> *This is my will. So mote it be.*

Then wrap the book in silk and keep it in its secret place to ripen until the time of the New Moon (when the moon is dark in the sky). On the New Moon, dedicate your book to the service of Our Lady.

## To Charge and Energize Your Tool

First, cast a sacred circle. Brush your book symbolically with a sweet-smelling twig. Place your book on your altar and sprinkle it with holy water (water and sea salt that you have dedicated to the service of Deity). Say:

> *Blessed Be, thou creature of ART. I dedicate you to the service of the Goddess,*
> *that She may form you. Words of Honor, Words of Truth, enter this tool and*
> *be obedient to Her, that She may guide you in purity and lead you to the path*
> *She has chosen for me. I charge you from the Center of Existence, above and*
> *below, throughout and about, within and without. I charge you to serve me in*
> *my service of the Goddess, between the worlds, and in all worlds. I charge you*
> *to be part of the One. So mote it be.*

Visualize the light blue aura of your sacred circle entering the book. Continue visualizing until you see the light absorbed into the book. When you are satisfied that, in your mind's eye, you have seen the light enter the book, say:

*This is my will. So mote it be.*

## Using Your Tool

Dedicate both your book and the pen that you will use to write in it. After you have dedicated your tools, you will be able to use them for your conversations with Deity. Treat this book and its pen as sacred objects and charge them to keep you safely within Her arms.

Always remember, a step on the path of the Craft of the Wise is not tread lightly. When you call your Creator, She will answer. If you dedicate this tool to Her, and treat it with respect and honor, She will speak to you in ways that reveal the Deity Within and the Self-which-is-Divine. She will teach you methods to stand in the face of adversity, bend with the winds of change, and march to the beat of your own drummer. She will guide your hand as you write. Your earnest work to know your self will be blessed.

As you begin to write, say these words out loud:

> *Wild and Free as Nature chose*
> > *Be the child your Mother knows*
> > > *Live the Life She set for you.*
> > > > *Be Thou True.*

> *RUN dot Child, and know your heart*
> > *You and I are not apart*
> > > *Joined as One we cannot tear,*
> > > > *I'll be there.*

> *RUN dot Child, we all are One*
> > *Interspersed with love and fun,*
> > > *When you find your special way,*
> > > > *"I'll" be there.*

And may your Book of Dreams and Shadows reveal the Divine in you.

Blessed be,
Lady Raya

---

Learn the full dedication ceremony and use of a witch's tool as described in Lady Raya's book, *13 Lessons for Pleasing the Divine: A Witch's Primer*, published by Weiser Books.

For a schedule of Moon phases and other information about the Craft, visit Lady Raya's website at: http://www.LadyRaya.org/

Last night I dreampt that I was with Carry and another girl. We were going to a party at this girls friends house. We got caught and ended up at a dress shop with 50 cent. I tried on a huge black dress and it made me look like a giant black marshmallow. At some point in the dream everyone abandoned me, I couldn't find them anywhere. Then we were sitting in Carry's car and she was going to drive 50 cent and a woman home. It was very weird.

## Summer Solstice

- fire source → candle
- divination tool - tarot cards
- rain water/dew (night ~~water~~ before
- white candle.
- 9 herbs

find
grapevines +
gold ribbon

## July 12

last night i had a dream that
lynx was alive again. i came home
and he was lying on my bed, quite
a few years younger, cleaning himself.
i yelled and picked him up and hugged
him. dylan or dad came in and said
'he came out of the ground yesterday.
said he didn't like being dead. reckon
he missed us.' then lynx licked me.

## August 26

I dreampt a while ago that i was in a van
with my parents. i was talking and they
were silent, staring forward. i looked down and
everything was blue. i was in the ocean. a
huge humpback whale swam by, so i grabed
it's tail. it didn't like it so it came back
and nudged me. we played and i did it
twice more. then i was standing outside
the van and the whale was laying with
it's tail across it's belly in the first bench
seat. i open the door and his tail flops out.
mom looks at me and says 'there's a whale
in the car.' and looks out the window again.

## August 30

Last night i dreampt that i was walking
through a field because carry's car died. we
thought it was the way to riding. Going
down a hill i spot a moose and it
charges. i run two steps and then drop

o the ground. i can see the chuncky gravel of the path. i'm expecting it to tample me, out the hooves stop and carry is petting it. a man emerges and tells us to pet it's nuzzle. we do and it runs away. he starts talking, and suddenly i'm in a town with hotels and restaurants. i ask someone about their asana, then i'm looking for a room, but i can't find one. The last thing i remember is thinking of finding Katie Mac Dondald. in a shady hotel area.

## September 22

a while ago i fell asleep between classes. i was ~~having a hard~~ walking around brock. it didn't look like any part that i've seen, but i knew it was brock. the middle blanks out out just before i woke up i remember being in a room with red velvet couches, with my parents. we were watching t.v., but we weren't paying attention to it. i was trying to talk to dad, but he ignored me. i was trying to get him to look at me. he pushed me out of the way, and sat down with mom. i hit my head on something. i was yelling 'dad! dad! why did you knock me over?' 'dad?' and then slowly got quietter. then my head started to throb. i woke up and said 'dad.' and started crying. the dream made me sad.

Feb 22 2005
in this dream. the entire robson side of
the family is running, or traveling somewhere.
we all seem to be in the gear over old
camping trips across the west. we all
had to catch a train (with large
baggage and cars.) i was holding a baby,
that got switched with someone elses.

November 23
il was in a house with familiar
people that i had to protect from
something. And for somereason. i had ually
brown skin

Dec. 3
i had a dream i was in a house, i
don't know where. living my daily.
life. But there were other people i
didn't recognize. And i think i had a
gun. maybe something about an assassin

Dec. 8
il dreampt that me, trish + amy (is an unnamed
guy) were driving around in a car talking
intil we got to a really old house. we
walked around it. There was really
good music.

Jan. 11   5:30 am

I just had the most vivid dream that
Cristina was lying on my bed with me and
we were talking and then she suddenly said
"Beth, I've realized that you're stupid and
all you do is condense information."
And from then on was horrible. I was angry
I cried a lot. I took a train home and
squatted in the snow and watch the people
changing trains. there was the ugliest two headed
boy that was talking that committed a
horrid crime. I closed a commplicated set
of blinds. And I woke up.

Cristina was standing in the ~~toor~~ bathroom.
and I asked her if she thought I was
stupid and she gave me a hug and said no.
It just hurt so much that she said it.

There was another part where I talked to
Steph. I called Cristina a Gestapo in my
anger. And Steph commented on an e-mail she sent
and how she tought that, Amy, I read it and then out
tried to get Trish & ~~Steph~~ to be more sympathotic
to her.

april 27th 2006

i had the strangest dream last night.
i was sitting in the livingroom of this
house, on the green couch with with my
computer in front of me. People were walking
through the house, can't remember who.
All of a sudden Prof. Kennedy came in.
He wandered around, suddenly the house
wasn't the same any more all of the
archetechture was different. We sat back
on the couch and i think we were talking
suddenly he kisses me on the mouth
and sits back stunned. then he said
something about being Catholic and not
being able to leave his wife. i think i might
have said it didn't matter... then i kissed him
on the lips and he got all nervous about
being caught. then i woke up.

october 30

i had a dream i was in an old
building with big windows, and
there is a kind of party going on.
i'm cantoodling with andy for the
majority of the dream until he leaves
and my 'boyfriend' who i like equally
and looks really Spainish shows up.
we hug and kiss and say i miss
you, but i'm thinking 'how can the
people at this party let me do this?'

november 20 2006
i had a dream amy, andy and i were
somewhere at a mall talking + hanging out
when this wrinkly woman with a blond
streak in her curly brown hair comes up.
it's his wife. amy and i stare wide-eyed
at each other and turn slowly and walk
away.

january 13 2007
in my dream, allison and i were at my house
in etobicoke and my entire family was there.
~~it~~ ally and i were getting ready to leave
to go somewhere when my dad tells me i
have to write something on a card for
one of mom's side's family friend. i blow
up and yell at my father for not telling
me before i had to go. i think he may have
seemed to be really impatient or something.
after arguing for a second and dylan
in the background giving me greif, i go
~~inside~~ inside to write my piece. it's
a ~~bun~~ bunch of cue cards in a long plastic
holder, there are notes from everyone, even
an old one from me that i remove +
replace. there is a picture of the couple,
in black and white on their wedding ~~day~~
and i stare at ~~of~~ it for a minute.
i think about what i want to say, and
write down 'the only thing we can hope to
find in this life are true friends + family.'

feb. 20 2007

a few days ago i had a dream that i was at home sitting at the dining room table talking to my mom. i had brought my boyfriend with me and 2 others. my mom was discussing him not being able to sleep in the same bed as me. this brought me major comfort, i can remember feeling elated, almost relieved. then she says that this time it doesn't matter and i panic. i filled with dread and woke up.

May 23 2007

last night i dreampt my hair was shorn completely from my head. it hung in differing lengths about my skull in the most unattractive of fashions. i was beside myself with pain + anguish over my lost locks. i cannot remember if it where I or another who so shamefully removed me of my hair.

june 27 2007

i dreampt amy leah + i were sitting on the median on the bridge to Brock. As a car drives by it looks like its going to hit this little tan/dun coloured weiner-dog. he sprints by us. i yell 'come here sweetie' and amy starts calling it loser. i get up to try and catch it. a woman in a van stops, she's a pet lady from the 'humain' society she tells me somehow he's in a lot of pain after i catch him. he's snuggled down in my arms when she injects him with something. she says 'don't worry, it'll take the pain away.' i watch his eyes close and wake up crying.

# confession

july 5 2007

this morning my bike was stolen out of our backyard. at first i was furious because someone had taken something from me. then i realized it was karma. i've been stealing tea from teaopia. it's because i've been stealing that someone has stolen from me. the tea will be throne out and never drank because its tainted. i will never steal again.
so mote it be. ✪

august 13 2007

lately i've been having many dreams, that are quite complex, but also fragmented. There was one in which i was in a house, a very large herse with lots of floors and rooms. there was also a family who lived there, and i think rented out rooms. wherever i went i always felt like i was intruding, like the people there had something to hide.
i had another dream of riding a large black horse through a muddy country lane. there where wheel marks in the mud filled with murky water. the saddle blanket is white, the saddle brown leather. i see his mane flying as he gallops. The brown braided reins are short. and pulled tight. greenary rushes by as i say 'whoa damon' and think demon. he slows but i want him to keep running. my phone rings and wakes me
i've had other dreams about harry potter also, though i can't remember the details
i remember wanting badly to slip back into the dream with demon. a strange longing for a ~~horse~~ horse.

august 15 2007

this morning i woke up feeling as if i had to, there
was a reason. in my dream i remember an elaborat
room with a semi circular couch. there was a knife
at some point, and a creepy guy. he was smarmy
and followed me around. there was another person
there, a friendly presence, but i never really saw her.
at some point the creeper started chasing me. i think
rape could have been the intention but i'm not
sure.

i couldn't get back to sleep for a long time after
and kept thinking about harry potter characters
mostly sirius black.


august 17 2007

i had a dream carry and i went to a really busy
mall and ordered mcdonalds. there was a giant
line up and racheal mcadams from mean girl
at cash. we all ordered food and something
happened and i got distracted. we end up at
a bar. i'm sitting at a table with carry. i
think i have one drink. people are milling
around everywhere. we're back at the hotel
room. there is a cott alongside 2 double
beds. i climb in the cott and ask carry
(whose getting into bed with another girl.
the other bed is also occupied, i'm not sure
who by) i ask he what she's done with my
food. she tells me she gave it to some guy.
i freak out and tell her she's the worst
friend in the world, and that i don't have
enough money to be giving away ten dollar meals.
her face crumples and starts to cry while
she's laying down. i turn and lay down facing
the wall fuming.

august 18 2007

i had a dream nat and i were on a trip in
Russia. we met lots of people speaking in
Russian on cold snowy streets. its was
definately a tourist trip. we went to malls
and such. at one point i was sitting at a
table waiting for nat to return, but carry
showed up carrying an apple bag. i wasn't
suprised to see her, all i thought was
'god, i hope its not an ipod!' and i woke
up confused that it wasn't nat who returned.

august 30 2007

i dreampt andy was over. we'd been together all
day. something, some kind of comotion happened
out side, and andy told me not to go out side.
i did anyways. when i came back in he was
in the shower. he came out into my room and said
he was drawing me a bath, and we got in it ~~togheat~~
together. he hugged me and i felt safe in his
arms. when he'd gotten out of the shower he shaved
me his shaved naked cock.
- while i was outside my phone kept ringing but no
names came up on the id, so i wouldn't answer it.

september 1 2007

i dreampt i heard leah through my clock radio.
she was talking to me through it. the last
thing i said was 'you aren't back with marty
are you!?' she sounded hesitant and asked why
i said 'cause i know you.' suddenly she's in
my room. i get up and we start talking. i must
have said something about him being an ass. then
told her she had to come to work. we started
arguing. right after i said something there
was this huge ball of stuff ~~in~~ in my mouth
and it grossed me right out. i started
spiting it out in the garbage and woke up.

november 3 2007

this morning i dreampt of allison leaving. i was standing watching her pack. she had a very unhappy look on her face. people were around us talking and someone made her keep packing. i kept telling her i didn't want her to go. i woke up crying, i was crying in my dream, i really didn't want her to leave. i'm going to miss her so much!

3